CONTEMPORARY CLOZE

Written by George Moore

GW00502648

Prim-Ed Publishing

www.prim-ed.com

Titles in this series:

LOWER (1st/2nd Class)

0661

MIDDLE (3rd/4th Class)

0662

UPPER (5th/6th Class)

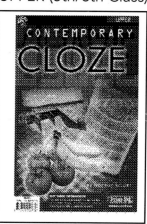

0663

0663IRE – 09/03

32/3

Foreword

Cloze is an effective teaching strategy widely used to assist in the development of reading and comprehension skills. Semantic and syntactic skills are developed as pupils use the context clues around the missing words in the text to make sense of each individual sentence.

As the title suggests, Contemporary Cloze – Upper covers a wide range of contemporary topics. These include up-to-date information about popular interests or themes, recent inventions or developments, and discussion about a selection of contemporary issues.

A variety of learning areas is covered including science, geography, technology, the arts, SPHE and physical education.

Other titles in this series:

Contemporary Cloze – Lower (1st/2nd Class)

Contemporary Cloze – Middle (3rd/4th Class)

The author wishes to thank his wife, Mary Moore, for her assistance during the writing of this book.

Contents

Teachers Notes

Contemporary Cloze provides pupils with the opportunity to practise using semantic and syntactic skills to assist in the development of reading and comprehension. Pupils use the context clues around the missing words in the text to make sense of individual sentences.

A variety of contemporary topics is covered including popular pupil interests or themes, recent inventions or developments, or discussion about a contemporary issue.

Teachers should be aware of the sensitivities of some pupils with topics such as 'cloning' or 'Xenotransplantation (Animal Organ Implants)'.

In some activities, pupils are provided with the list of missing words. After reading the text, pupils should sort out the obvious choices first and cross out the words as they are used.

Sometimes pupils will need to refer to a diagram, map or illustration to work out the missing word.

In other activities, pupils must choose their own words to complete the text. Again, pupils should sort out the obvious choices first. Pupils may choose different words to the answers provided. These may still be correct if used in the proper context.

The missing words may be a random selection or a specific group of words such as nouns, verbs, adjectives or adverbs.

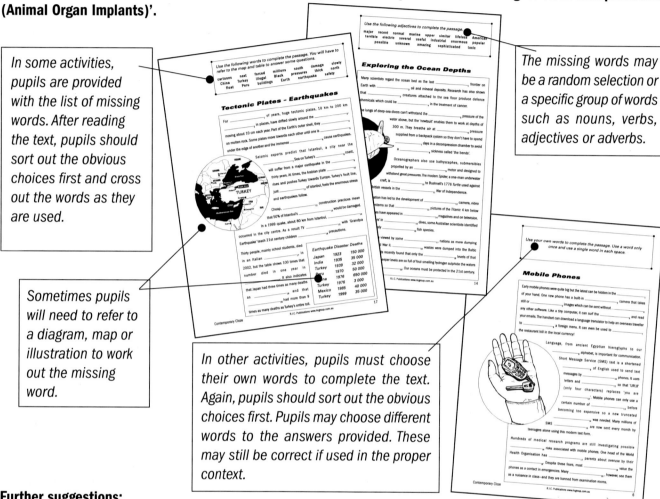

Further suggestions:

- The topic can be discussed with the whole class or in small groups before pupils complete the cloze activity.
- Some of the contemporary topics suggest further discussion following the completion of the activity. Reports by small research groups on particular topics could feature in a series of lessons.
- Unless teachers want to assess the ability of individual pupils, the cloze activities could be completed in pairs to enable an interchange of ideas. This works well with less capable readers, who could be partnered with a reader of the same ability or learn from a more capable pupil.
- Similarly, the activities could be enlarged and completed as a group or class. The teacher could model techniques to work out the missing words.
- Encourage the use of dictionaries to clarify the meaning of difficult words.
- Teachers could revise with the pupils a particular part of speech for the activities where a specific group of words in missing. These include:

Nouns	are naming words like 'dog', 'Africa', 'summer'.
Adjectives	are words which describe nouns or words which represent nouns (pronouns). Adjectives usually appear in front of the word they describe but can appear after that word: e.g. 'The boy is tall'.
Adverbs	add further meaning to a verb: e.g. 'She walked slowly down the road'. (How did she walk? slowly – adverb)
Verbs	used are 'action' words; e.g. 'run', 'fly', 'skate'.
Phrases	are groups of words which do not make sense by themselves. They do not contain a 'finite' verb (a verb with a subject; e.g. 'Callum ran home at once.' Who ran? Callum (subject)). The adverb 'phrases of place' answer the question 'Where?' and such phrases include 'near the door', 'on the desk', 'at home'.

Teachers Notes

Relevant background information has been included where necessary for each topic.

Curriculum Links

The activities within the three-book series *Contemporary Cloze* have been written to assist the development of reading and comprehension skills. The non-fiction cloze procedure activities are ideal for developing prediction strategies, encouraging children to predict, check, confirm and self-correct when reading.

The variety of cloze procedures in *Contemporary Cloze* will encourage children to demonstrate the following objectives of the English Language Revised Primary School Curriculum for Ireland.

Book	Strand	Strand Unit	Class	Content Objectives
Lower	Receptiveness to language	Reading	1st & 2nd	· develop reading skills through engaging with reading material appropriate to his/her stage of development
	Developing cognitive abilities through language	Reading	1st & 2nd	· develop comprehension strategies
	Emotional and imaginative development through language	Reading	1st & 2nd	· engage with a wide variety of text
Middle	Receptiveness to language	Reading	3rd & 4th	· use more than one strategy when reading unfamiliar text · become an increasingly independent reader
	Competence and confidence in using language	Reading	3rd & 4th	· experience different types of text
	Developing cognitive abilities through language	Reading	3rd & 4th	· continue to develop a range of comprehension strategies · use a knowledge of printing conventions as an aid to expression and comprehension
Upper	Receptiveness to language	Reading	5th & 6th	· achieve proficiency in word identification by refining different word identification skills
	Competence and confidence in using language	Reading	5th & 6th	· read widely as an independent reader from a more challenging range of reading material
	Developing cognitive abilities through language	Reading	5th & 6th	· use comprehension skills such as confirming and prediction

Use the following words to complete the passage.

journey companions Return destroying might twists found
voted regain screen again travelling language actors
wizard director forces struggle creation landscapes

The Lord of the Rings

The Lord of the Rings by the late J R R Tolkein, a _____1 professor at Oxford University, has been _____2 the best book of the 20th century in several worldwide polls. Now, in this century, film-making technology brings to the _____3 Tolkein's fantasy trilogy which concludes with The _____4 of the King. The many fantasy creatures such as Gollum and Treebeard were brought to life using actors and CGI (computer–generated imaging). With these amazing visual effects and using world-famous _____5 like Cate Blanchett and Elijah Wood, the films bring Tolkein's epic tale to entranced cinema-goers. The _____6, Peter Jackson, shot all the films back to back in New Zealand. There, the wide variety of _____7 imaginatively described in Tolkein's books could be _____8 without the enormous cost of _____9 around the world to different locations.

The story tells how Gandalf the _____10, Frodo the Hobbit and their _____11 set off on a dangerous journey across Middle Earth to save their people by _____12 the ring of power. They _____13 through many strange lands, constantly pursued by the _____14 of the Dark Lord, Sauron and the Creature, Gollum. Sauron and Gollum are both driven to _____15 possession of the ring. Sauron needs his _____16 to return to full power so he _____17 hold all Middle Earth under his control. Gollum desires once _____18 to have his 'precious' (the ring). The companions _____19 against both these foes and against the ring itself, that _____20 all it touches, and desires only to return to its creator, Sauron.

Use the following nouns to complete the passage.

paintings   centuries   tombs   lovers   elephants   government
insurance   Romans   film   room   University   world   paint
heroes   complaints   example   people   money   museums   surface

Changing Art

Ancient Egyptian art decorated _____₁ with images of an afterlife. Greek art depicted their gods and mythical _____₂ like Achilles and was admired by the _____₃ who copied it. In the 14th, 15th and 16th _____₄' religious paintings were of the greatest importance.

At one time, _____₅ had to travel to the world's art galleries and _____₆ to see great works of art. Nowadays—though security and _____₇ costs are huge—Rodin's sculptures, _____₈ by Titian and Constable or modernists like Ben Nicholson and Jackson Pollock travel the _____₉ in special exhibitions.

A recent _____₁₀, *Pollock,* reminds us of an Australian _____₁₁ which paid over €1.8 million for 'Blue Poles'. This is an _____₁₂ of Pollock's action painting where _____₁₃ is dripped or thrown onto a horizontal _____₁₄. Many people protested about the waste of taxpayer's _____₁₅—but it is now worth a great deal more!

Some modern sculptures, such as 'Lipstick Ascending on Caterpillar Tracks' at Yale _____₁₆, have outraged thousands of art _____₁₇. Britain's websites were flooded with _____₁₈ when the 2001 Turner Prize winner was a model of an empty _____₁₉ with a flickering light bulb! We even have popular exhibitions of paintings by _____₂₀ and chimpanzees! Van Gogh couldn't sell a painting while he was alive but now they are worth millions!

Child Stars

Shirley Temple, _____ [1] for her hit song *On the Good Ship, Lollipop,* made her _____ [2] film at the age of 3. Soon she'd become one of the most _____ [3] child stars of the last century. Drew Barrymore will always be remembered as the _____ [4] girl Gertie in *E.T.*, while Daniel Radcliffe is the popular schoolboy, Harry Potter. Macaulay Culkin starred in the _____ [5] film *Home Alone,* which made over €650 million in the 1990s.

Welsh girl Charlotte Church's CD, *Voice of an Angel,* made her the _____ [6] artist ever to reach No. 1 in the _____ [7] classical charts in 2002. She was a millionaire at 13 but only had a _____ [8] €18 a week pocket money from her very _____ [9] parents!

The North _____ [10] TV appearances of the Olsen twins, Mary-Kate and Ashley, at 9 months old, eventually led to a _____ [11] TV series. Soon, their enormous popularity created an _____ [12] supply of films, music, software, dolls, books and clothing. Their _____ [13] income is estimated at over one billion euro!

Child stardom obviously has its _____ [14] rewards but no privacy for the _____ [15] star. Fame for some of them has led to _____ [16] squabbles with parents or disagreements with _____ [17] managers over money. Judy Garland led a _____ [18] life after starring in *The Wizard of Oz,* one of the _____ [19] children's films. Perhaps we should be grateful we lead _____ [20] lives!

Use your own words to complete the passage. Use one word in each space and do not use the same word more than once.

The Family Car

Safety developments like seatbelts and _____1 for a world with millions of cars are very _____2 because of the high road death toll. Japanese engineers are _____3 with instruments which can control the car when the driver _____4 a heart attack or faints. Research on 'stop/go' systems which keep the car a _____5 distance from other drivers in heavy traffic are also being _____6.

Tiny interior cameras which detect driver fatigue are being _____7 in Australia and many car companies are interested. Tired eyes will activate a recorded _____8 telling the driver to take care or the system will cause the seat to _____9. Initially, this 'Facelab' system will _____10 about €45 000, but in time should be a lot less.

Unlike normal plastics, which are petroleum-based, Japan has _____11 car parts using starch from sweet potatoes _____12 with natural fibres. This biodegradable 'bioplastic' mixture will _____13 break down naturally and be less harmful to our environment.

Los Angeles, a heavily polluted city, has _____14 to test several fuel cell cars which use hydrogen to power their electric _____15 and are rated 'zero emission vehicles'. The five-million-euro Hy-wire_____16, tested in Monaco in 2002, is powered by a fuel-cell. With a big _____17 space where the engine should be and a clear plastic bumper, drivers have a fascinating _____18 of the road ahead. Vehicles which _____19 petrol with electric power, 'hybrids', are also environmentally friendly and _____20 are planning to produce many more.

Use the following words to complete the passage. You will need to refer to the diagram to fill in some of the spaces.

airports　called　moving　cheaper　roof　metres　air
differ　litres　engines　private　built　huge　personal
deafening　up　Olympics　true　down　weight

Transport in the Future

Future modes of transport will _differ_ [1] from those used today. We could see film fantasies come ~~true~~ _true_ [2] with spaceships linking cities and citizens on _moving_ [3] 'travelators' winding round city streets. We may use airboards, _personal_ [4] hovercraft like those used in Sydney's _Olympics_ [5]. They ride on a cushion of _air_ [6] and are driven by a simple petrol engine. Airboards can only be used on _private_ [7] land at present as no laws cover them on public roads.

Some cargo planes are _huge_ [8], but Boeing engineers have plans for an even larger cargo plane _called_ [9] the Pelican. Its wingspan is 150 _metres_ [10], the wings slope _down_ [11], it has four _engines_ [12] and is twice the size of the Russian AN 225. The Pelican's _weights_ [13] would prevent it taking off from Starrports, which are possible future _airports_ [14], named after their designer, Jim Starry. Planes take off from a Starrport's _roof_ [15], then along a shortened runway with a 1% slope. The slope means a Jumbo jet would save over 1 300 _litres_ [16] of fuel. When landing _up_ [17] the slope, gravity halts the plane with huge fuel savings and no need for the _deafening_ [18] reverse thrust of the engines.

Sea travel, once _cheaper_ [19] than air travel, will see even bigger cruise ships carrying thousands of passengers. In 2002, forty-two new ships were being _built_ [20], some weighing over 100 000 tonnes!

Mobile Phones

Early mobile phones were quite big but the latest can be hidden in the _____₁ of your hand. One new phone has a built-in _____₂ camera that takes still or _____₃ images which can be sent without _____₄ any other software. Like a tiny computer, it can surf the _____₅ and read your emails. The handset can download a language translator to help an overseas traveller to _____₆ a foreign menu. It can even be used to _____₇ the restaurant bill in the local currency!

Language, from ancient Egyptian hieroglyphs to our _____₈ alphabet, is important for communication. Short Message Service (SMS) text is a shortened _____₉ of English used to send text messages by _____₁₀ phones. It uses letters and _____₁₁ so that 'URL8' (only four characters) replaces 'you are _____₁₂'. Mobile phones can only use a certain number of _____₁₃ before becoming too expensive so a new truncated _____₁₄ was needed. Many millions of SMS _____₁₅ are now sent every month by teenagers alone using this modern text form.

Hundreds of medical research programmes are still investigating possible _____₁₆ risks associated with mobile phones. One head of the World Health Organisation has _____₁₇ parents about overuse by their _____₁₈. Despite these fears, most _____₁₉ value the phones as a contact in emergencies. Many _____₂₀ , however, see them as a nuisance in class—and they are banned from examination rooms.

Use the following words to complete the poem. The poem uses rhyming couplets which means that each pair of successive lines end in rhyming words.

ease games school peers tall see lose beware TV schools all
rules tears aware names tease choose outside cruel denied

Bullying

Of bullying today we are more _____1'

Schools have strategies, so bullies _____2!

Taunting, abuse and calling _____3

The bully's excuse—just playing _____4!

We picture the bully as strong and _____5

But that may not be the culprit at _____6'

Frail-looking bullies can slyly _____7

Their nasty tales make pupils ill at _____8'

They can isolate socially someone they _____9

So these lonely targets have friends they can _____10

The bully—poor role models, outside of _____11?

Conditioned by elders both unfair and _____12?

Perhaps they don't fit in, or there's pressure from _____13

Is that an excuse to reduce classmates to _____14?

Do they view these examples in films, on _____15?

Is it aggressive behaviours we want them to _____16?

Parents and teachers should discuss forming _____17'

Work hard to discourage this scourge in our _____18'

Make school policies known in school and _____19

So each pupil's rights cannot be _____20.

Use your own words to complete the passage. Select one word for each space and do not use a word more than once.

Body Image

Recent studies _____1 that attractive children are popular with classmates and _____2 at school, and attractive job applicants have a _____3 chance of success. This 'bias for beauty' is even _____4 in our literature—wicked stepmothers or cruel sisters are _____5 but good fairies are beautiful.

TV commercials, magazines and films show images of handsome stars or _____6 models. The slimness of many models is _____7 to achieve for the average adult or teenager, so low self-esteem may _____8 to anorexia or bulimia, both _____9 to a person's health. Men are less self-critical, with _____10 of hair and lack of height _____11 of their main worries.

Recent studies in America and Sweden found many primary _____12 girls had dieted in order to _____13 weight and almost half of Japanese primary pupils _____14 they were too fat. Boys are less critical of their _____15 except during adolescence. Any teasing of their appearance when young may permanently affect children's _____16 image but school educational programmes can help _____17 to accept who they are.

'Beauty is in the eye of the beholder' said Margaret Hungerford and perceptions vary from culture to _____18. 'Giraffe' women with metal bands wrapped _____19 elongated necks or other native women with a large plate stretching their lower lip are _____20 attractive within their own culture.

Limited Overs Cricket

The first one-day game was _____1 in England in 1963 and then introduced to international _____2. It has gained enormous popularity and has been the _____3 source of revenue for the countries _____4. In cricket-mad India it has become far more _____5 than Test cricket and new competitors like Bangladesh, Zimbabwe and Kenya are now _____6 of the world programme. Outstanding _____7 such as Adam Gilchrist, Sachin Tendulkar and Brian Lara have _____8 of fans around the globe. Women also play this _____9 of the game and Australia's Belinda Clark has a record score of 229 not out for a one-day _____10.

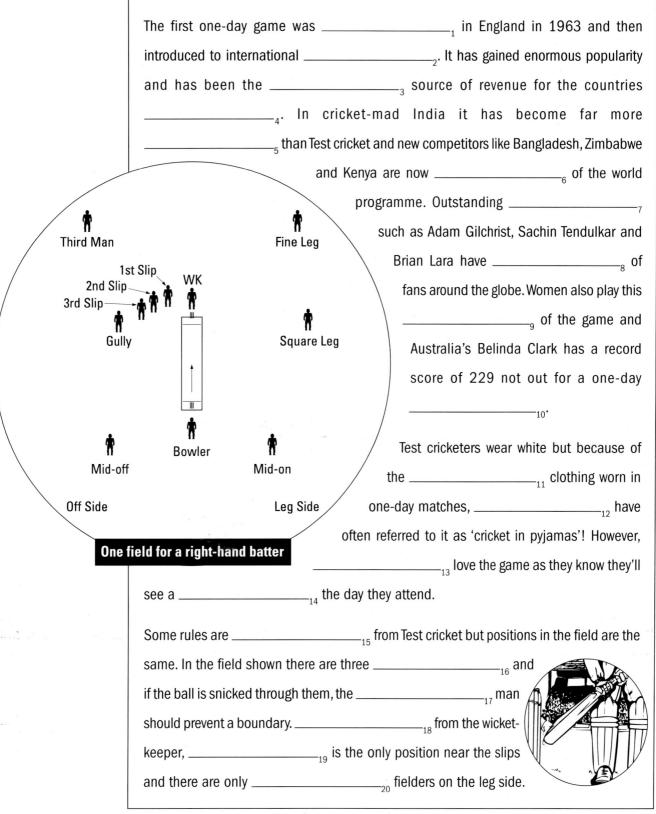

One field for a right-hand batter

Test cricketers wear white but because of the _____11 clothing worn in one-day matches, _____12 have often referred to it as 'cricket in pyjamas'! However, _____13 love the game as they know they'll see a _____14 the day they attend.

Some rules are _____15 from Test cricket but positions in the field are the same. In the field shown there are three _____16 and if the ball is snicked through them, the _____17 man should prevent a boundary. _____18 from the wicket-keeper, _____19 is the only position near the slips and there are only _____20 fielders on the leg side.

Use the following adjectives to complete the passage.

~~several~~ ~~high-rise~~ ~~individual~~ ~~broken~~ ~~serious~~ local ~~obvious~~ ~~physical~~ ~~Extreme~~ ~~various~~ ~~important~~ ~~dangerous~~ ~~long~~ particular ~~in-line~~ ~~greatest~~ ~~firm~~ ~~artificial~~ ~~every~~ ~~increasing~~

Extreme Sports

Extreme (1) sports include excitement, skills and danger with *Physical* (2) activities below ground, in the air and on the water. Most are *individual* (3) sports rather than team events, with participants trying to avoid the *obvious* (4) dangers but enjoying the thrills. Sydney's 2000 Olympics was for the *greatest* (5) athletes, but in December 2002 Sydney also hosted the Planet X Games for Extreme Sports stars from *various* (6) parts of the world.

Base jumping—that is, parachuting from *high-rise* (7) buildings, bridges etc.—is the most *dangerous* (8) of these sports which include hang-gliding, BMX, *in-line* (9) skating, skateboarding and surfing. One skateboarder in 1998 was timed at 100 km/h and *every* (10) year doctors treat thousands of youngsters for *broken* (11) bones or fractures, with spinal injuries from surfing accidents adding to the *long* (12) injury list. Quality protective equipment is very *important* (13), especially helmets to protect the head and *firm* (14) shin or elbow pads to prevent *serious* (15) abrasions.

Authorities in *several* (16) countries have built bike tracks, skateboard facilities or *artificial* (17) surfing reefs to cater for the *increasing* (18) popularity of extreme sports. If you'd like to read more about a *particular* (19) extreme sport, you only need to look in your *local* (20) newsagency. There you will find an array of magazines catering for extreme sport enthusiasts.

Use the following words to complete the passage.

supplies   roads   technology   expensive   lifted   reduces
regulations   cartons   bacteria   drunk   food   household   small
required   paper   recycled   fires   Europe   washes   find

Recycling

By recycling _____₁ we save our trees, but we can also recycle glass bottles,

milk _____₂ and plastic. Recycling conserves many non-renewable

resources and _____₃ greenhouse gas emissions because local councils

send less _____₄ waste to landfill sites. It also means less energy is

_____₅ when making new materials from old.

Health _____₆ once prevented recycled plastic

from being used for _____₇ containers but

new   technology   has   seen   this   ban

_____₈ in some countries.

Sewage   and   stormwater   collected   from

_____₉ and the roofs of buildings, is

also _____₁₀. Water treatment plants

treat   millions   of   litres   a   day,   removing

_____₁₁ and unwanted particles. This

recycled water can't be _____₁₂ or used

for   cooking   but   is   able   to   be   used   for   car

_____₁₃, flushing toilets, watering parks and fighting

_____₁₄. This means there is a reduced demand on drinking water

_____₁₅.

New _____₁₆ is constantly improving

recycling techniques in _____₁₇,

America   and   Japan,   but   countries   with

_____₁₈ populations like Australia or

Belgium may _____₁₉ these new

developments are too _____₂₀ to use in

the immediate future.

Use the following verbs to complete the passage.

searched   assemble   led   Equipped   destroyed   solve   distinguish
produced   weld   approach   find   interacts   are   walked
programmed   recognises   reacts   mow   understand   driven

Robots

Recent developments in electronics and computer technology have _____1 to important advances in robotics. Humanoids _____2 human-like machines with mechanical arms and legs. In 2001, secret research by Japan's Honda company _____3 one the size of a 10-year-old child. Guided by remote control, it _____4 and could grasp objects.

Today, one-armed industrial robots are used to _____5 and spraypaint car body parts, and some can even _____6 electronic circuits and tiny parts in watches. The different movements required are _____7 into the robot's memory. Robots are also used to _____8 and defuse terrorist bombs. _____9 with cameras and electronic touch sensors, three small robots similar to remote-control model cars _____10 for victims among the rubble of New York's Twin Towers after the terrorist attack _____11 them.

'Kismet', _____12 by 15 computers, is the world's first robot which _____13 with people because it _____14 their moods through the varying pitch of their speech. Though it can't _____15 what is said, Kismet recognises a sad or angry voice and _____16 to it with appropriate gestures.

Though future robots will _____17 our lawns and vacuum our homes, engineers _____18 that designing a robot even to _____19 an egg from a book or bottle is still a major problem to _____20.

High-speed Trains

Since the days of George Stephenson's 1829 *Rocket*, a steam locomotive, engineers have tried to _____₁ faster trains. The world's fastest trains using _____₂ wheels, modified tracks and overhead _____₃ have been France's TGV (*trains a la grande vitesse*) and Japan's 'bullet trains'.

Engineers around the world have been developing high-speed _____₄ levitation trains ('maglevs') and an early Japanese test model, ML-500, has _____₅ over 500 km/h. One type of maglev has an electrodynamic system and glides _____₆ the track using magnetic repulsion—seen when the 'like' poles of two _____₇ repel each other in classroom experiments. Magnets on the underside of the maglev create _____₈ in wire coils or metal plates set in the track (the 'guideway'). The _____₉ is lifted about 10 cm above the guideway by the opposing magnetic forces. The moving currents push the train forward like ocean _____₁₀ pushing a surfer along. Another type of maglev uses electromagnetic forces where magnetic _____₁₁ rather than repulsion is used.

In 2003, a new high-speed maglev linked Shanghai _____₁₂ to the city, but tickets are very _____₁₃. In the not too distant future, maglev trains travelling at 500 km/h are _____₁₄ to compete with planes on some routes and Germany and _____₁₅ already use low-speed maglevs. Because there is no _____₁₆ with the guideway, the rides are very smooth and _____₁₇. As there is no surface-to-surface friction, the guideways need little _____₁₈ and because maglevs use electric _____₁₉, there is a minimal pollution of the _____₂₀.

Use the following adjectives to complete the passage.

major   recent   normal   marine   upper   similar   lifeless   American
terrible   electric   several   useful   industrial   enormous   popular
possible   unknown   amazing   sophisticated   toxic

Exploring the Ocean Depths

Many scientists regard the ocean bed as the last _____1 frontier on Earth with _____2 oil and mineral deposits. Research has also shown that _____3 creatures attached to the sea floor produce defence chemicals which could be _____4 in the treatment of cancer.

The lungs of deep-sea divers can't withstand the _____5 pressure of the water above, but the 'newtsuit' enables them to work at depths of 300 m. They breathe air at _____6 pressure supplied from a backpack system so they don't have to spend _____7 days in a decompression chamber to avoid a _____8 sickness called 'the bends'.

Oceanographers also use bathyscaphes, submersibles propelled by an _____9 motor and designed to withstand great pressures. The modern *Spider,* a one-man underwater craft, is _____10 to Bushnell's 1776 *Turtle* used against British vessels in the _____11 War of Independence.

Ocean exploration has led to the development of _____12 camera, video and lighting systems so that _____13 pictures of the *Titanic* 4 km below the Atlantic waves have appeared in _____14 magazines and on television. Using 'deep rovers' in _____15 dives, some Australian scientists identified over 700 previously _____16 fish species.

Oceans have been viewed by some _____17 nations as mere dumping grounds. After World War II, _____18 wastes were dumped into the Baltic Sea. Marine scientists recently found that only the _____19 levels of that sea contain oxygen. Deeper levels are so full of foul-smelling hydrogen sulphide the waters are virtually _____20. Our oceans must be protected in the 21st century.

Protecting Our Borders

Customs officers have _____1 tried to detect those people who _____2 try to break a country's border laws, which are _____3 enforced. These offenders are _____4 caught smuggling in the seeds of banned plants or _____5 concealing exotic creatures to sell overseas. A rare parrot or lizard can _____6 be sold for thousands of euro. Only _____7, a man flying from Melbourne to Vienna tried _____8 to smuggle 60 geckos in a trade which _____9 seeks profit and shows no interest in _____10 protecting unique wildlife. Offenders can be _____11 fined, over €60 000 sometimes, and _____12 given jail sentences. We all know drugs _____13 affect so many lives and some Asian countries have very severe penalties for those who _____14 try to smuggle drugs through their Customs.

Since the 2001 _____15 brutal terrorist attack on New York and the Bali bombs in 2002, Customs departments worldwide have _____16 increased the number of sniffer dogs able to detect explosives. Many airports and seaports have teams of _____17 trained dogs which can _____18 detect over 19 000 explosives combinations!

_____19, new X-ray machines with a much improved capacity will reduce the chances of smuggling explosives, weapons or drugs into the country to _____20 nil.

Use the following words to complete the passage. You will need to use the graph to fill in some of the spaces.

graph   populations   responsible   emissions   India   paying
changes   temperature   Canada   trees   annually   rise   aim
countries   support   thirty-six   America   Japan   country   earnt

Global Warming

The Kyoto Pact, developed in Kyoto, Japan, in 1997, aimed to cut _____₁ of the greenhouse gas carbon dioxide, which some scientists blame for raising the Earth's _____₂. Research alleges 'global warming' has led to a thinner Arctic icecap. Scientists who _____₃ the greenhouse gas theory predict sea levels could _____₄ by almost a metre this century and threaten _____₅ in low-lying areas. Other scientists see current higher temperature levels as a part of natural cyclical _____₆ which are not influenced by humans and which have always affected us.

The updated pact has now been signed by many _____₇, including high-emission Asian nations such as Japan, China and _____₈. The original pact had to be approved by any group of nations _____₉ for at least 55% of the 1990 emissions. The _____₁₀ shows America's contribution was _____₁₁%, four times the emissions from _____₁₂ and twelve times the percentage for _____₁₃.

Percentages of CO₂ emissions from industrial countries in 1990

Canada
Australia and New Zealand
Eastern Europe
Japan
Russia
European Union
US

0   5   10   15   20   25   30   35
percentages

If industrial nations can't reduce their emissions, they can at least plant _____₁₄, as just one hectare of forest can absorb over 100 tonnes of carbon _____₁₅. These 'carbon credits' can be _____₁₆ by planting trees in their own country or _____₁₇ another government to plant in their available areas.

In 2002, _____₁₈, said to be the worst polluter, had not signed the pact, as President Bush said it was against the 'economic best interests' of his _____₁₉. However, perhaps the best outcome for the entire planet should be the world's _____₂₀ in this century!

Use the following words to complete the passage. You will have to refer to the map and table to answer some questions.

cartoons	next	forced	millions	south	damage	slowly
China	Turkey	illegal	Black	pressures	thick	north
float	Peru	buildings	Earth	earthquake	safety	

Tectonic Plates – Earthquakes

For _____₁ of years, huge tectonic plates, 10 km to 200 km _____₂ in places, have drifted slowly around the _____₃' moving about 10 cm each year. Part of the Earth's outer shell, they _____₄ on molten rock. Some plates move towards each other until one is _____₅ under the edge of another and the immense _____₆ cause earthquakes.

Seismic experts predict that Istanbul, a city near the _____₇ Sea on Turkey's _____₈ coast, will suffer from a major earthquake in the _____₉ thirty years. At times, the Arabian plate _____₁₀ rises and pushes Turkey towards Europe. Turkey's fault line, just _____₁₁ of Istanbul, feels the enormous stress and earthquakes follow.

Cheap, _____₁₂ construction practices mean that 50% of Istanbul's _____₁₃ would be damaged. In a 1999 quake, about 80 km from Istanbul, _____₁₄ occurred in the city centre. As a result TV _____₁₅ with 'Grandpa Earthquake' teach 21st century children _____₁₆ precautions.

Thirty people, mainly school pupils, died in an Italian _____₁₇ in 2002, but the table shows 100 times that number died in one year in _____₁₈. It also indicates that Japan had three times as many deaths as _____₁₉ and that _____₂₀ had more than 20 times as many deaths as Turkey's entire toll.

Map labels: UKRAINE, RUMANIA, Bucharest, BULGARIA, Sofia, Black Sea, GEORGIA, Byzantium, Istanbul, ARMENIA, Ankara, Fault line, TURKEY, GREECE, Athens, Zeugma, SYRIA, Lebanon, CYPRUS, Damascus, IRAQ, Mediterranean Sea, Cairo

Earthquake Disaster Deaths		
Japan	1923	150 000
India	1935	35 000
Turkey	1939	32 000
Peru	1970	50 000
China	1976	650 000
Turkey	1976	3 000
Mexico	1985	40 000
Turkey	1999	35 000

Use the following verbs to complete the passage.

import   soak   performed   found   attempted   producing   help
turn   provide   opened   fix   want   depend   put
water   possessed   predicts   lies   collect   survive

Water is Precious

Water is _____1 in huge quantities on the Earth's surface and underground, but most _____2 in salty oceans or frozen glaciers and icecaps. Only about 1% is useable fresh water. UNESCO _____3 that by 2020 there will be a worldwide shortage. In past years, people _____4 rain dances and scientists around the world 'seeded' dark clouds with chemicals as they _____5 to bring rain.

Now, desalination plants worldwide _____6 seawater into quality drinking water. Saudi Arabia's plants _____7 the country with a liquid more precious than its oil, for people can _____8 weeks without food but only a few days without water.

Some areas in Australia can't _____9 gardens with sprinklers during most daylight hours. Parts of California _____10 on winter rains and during droughts they have to _____11 expensive water from the Colorado River. Some American coastal cities are considering desalination plants and Tampa, Florida, _____12 America's first major plant in 2003, _____13 over 100 million litres of water a day. These cities _____14 sufficient water supplies but huge population increases _____15 pressure on resources, and nowadays more people _____16 automatic washing machines, second bathrooms, spas and so on.

Families can _____17 at home: replace lawns, which can _____18 up 50% of domestic water, with drought-resistant plants; use half flushes in toilets; _____19 leaky taps; take short showers and use a bucket to _____20 excess shower water! Every drop helps!

Use the following words to complete the passage. You will need to use the map to complete some of the answers.

drainage   Brazil   salts   occurs   Colorado   China   areas
Tigris   Ethiopia   years   available   problem   remove   volunteers   Egypt
watertable   vegetation   Victoria   Indonesia   notice

Salinity

Salt _____1 naturally in soil and poses no _____2 until people upset nature's balance. Thousands of _____3 ago the Sumerians salinated the soil near the Euphrates and _____4 rivers by inappropriate agricultural practices.

Clearing deep-rooted native _____5 to grow shallow-rooted crops which don't use all the _____6 ground water, causes the watertable to rise. This brings soluble _____7 closer to the surface, which in turn inhibit plant growth. _____8 in South America, Australia and near neighbour _____9, are still clearing huge _____10 of natural vegetation. In Australia, _____11 plant millions of trees, and deep drains and aquifer pumps are also used to _____12 excess groundwater.

Areas of severe salinity

Overuse of irrigation water also raises the _____13 especially in areas with poor _____14. Salinity is slow and silent; it may be 25 years before farmers _____15 that their trees are dying.

Millions of hectares worldwide are affected: the state of _____16 in the USA; salt crusts on farmland in _____17, the Sudan and _____18 on the African continent; problems near the Yellow River in _____19; and Western Australia and the states of NSW and _____20 in Australia have problems.

Salt eventually kills plants.

Salty water

Watertable rises.

Use the following phrases to complete the passage. Phrases are groups of words which don't make complete sense by themselves. Each adverb phrase (of place) answers the question, 'Where?'.

inside homes	around the world	in the northern hemisphere
in power plants	in nearby Germany	around the local district
in the US Congress	on monuments	in scientific records
in many waterways	to affected water	in fish populations
in Asia	in Europe	in snow from fuels
from volcanoes	through the air	in the water in England

Acid Rain

The name 'acid rain' results from early atmospheric studies _____1.

Sulphuric and nitric acids are found in acid rain and _____2. Fossil fuels, oil and coal, burnt in factories and _____3, produce sulphur dioxide and nitrogen oxide which combine with water vapour to form acid rain.

Sulphur dioxide is spewed _____4 but the greatest threat comes from industrial emissions _____ _____5.

Anglers in Sweden noticed declines _____ _____6 and then Swedish scientists found that acidity _____7 was killing the fish. After further studies _____8, acid rain was blamed for the 'deaths' of thousands of lakes _____ _____9. Fish have disappeared from some North American lakes, and _____10 only bacteria and algae survive.

Sulphur dioxide travels _____11 and British emissions are thought to be polluting forests _____12.

Acid rain causes erosion _____13, bridges, statues and historic buildings of marble and limestone. Some sulphur can be removed _____14 but it is expensive. Many modern power stations build chimneys to minimise pollution _____15 but send the problem elsewhere.

Adding lime _____16 reduces acidity but can itself be harmful.

In 1990, politicians _____17 amended their *Clean Air Act* to reduce industrial emissions. By 2002, improvements were noticed _____ _____18 but there is a growing problem _____19 where China uses high-sulphur coal to generate electricity _____20.

Use the following words to complete the passage.

engineered   heart   extra   bees   starving   grown   donated
tomatoes   protests   Australia   dangerous   insect   Canada   milk
tastier   resistant   seeds   size   concern   supermarkets

Genetically Modified (GM) Foods

Lactic acid added to foods prevents _____1 bacteria developing, and fish oil added to milk can reduce _____2 disease. People accept these 'value-added foods', but GM foods still cause _____3 about long-term health effects so they need to be labelled in _____4. Low-cholesterol margarine is made from canola _____5, but now GM canola is produced in America and its neighbour _____6, while crops like wheat are being trialled in _____7. One problem is that GM pollen carried by winds or _____8 could affect nearby crops.

Fifty-three million hectares of GM crops were _____9 worldwide in 2002. They are similar to normal crops but possess an _____10 gene inserted by DNA technology; e.g. a gene that protects them from _____11 pests. Genes can also be removed and a gene which caused _____12 in California to break down was removed so _____13 tomatoes were then produced. A dahlia gene inserted into bananas will make them _____14 to the fungal disease siggatoka and an extra gene makes cows' _____15 more nutritious. GM salmon now grow to full _____16 in a quarter of the time after being _____17 with another fish's gene.

In 2002, Zambia discovered that the free maize _____18 by America was genetically engineered. Zambia's government then banned it, even though 3 000 000 Zambians were _____19! The European Union, where _____20 first started in Germany, also banned GM foods in the same year. It appears that the concerns are still present.

Use the following words to complete the passage.

criminal   successfully   phones   types   others   fluids   hair
analyse   police   cells   now   stream   sift   comparison
clearly   weapon   voluntarily   identify   programmes   traced

Forensic Science

Technology in forensic science is helping _____₁ forces to fight criminals more _____₂ and Melbourne University has the world's first forensic medicine centre. Modern tools include: computer _____₃ that change fuzzy surveillance tapes into _____₄-seen images; infra-red spectrometers which identify different _____₅ of ink used on ransom demands; _____₆ microscopes to scientifically compare bullets; chemical scanners that _____₇ evidence and very controversial sensors which _____₈ a suspect's brainwaves. Crime investigators can use electron microscopes to send a _____₉ of electrons on to material recently handled by a _____₁₀ so that, for example, any gunpowder from a _____₁₁ the suspect is accused of using can be identified.

Electron microscope

We _____₁₂ know that voiceprints from secretly tapped _____₁₃ are unique, like DNA and fingerprints, and can be _____₁₄ to an individual. DNA cells are extracted from _____₁₅ like sweat, tears and saliva, or from body tissues, in order to _____₁₆ a particular person. DNA is only found in _____₁₇ with a nucleus, so cells from teeth, fingernails and _____₁₈ are ruled out. Many prisoners have refused to _____₁₉ give up their DNA, but DNA samples have cleared _____₂₀ already serving sentences in prisons. Nevertheless, these technologies raise serious questions about rights to privacy.

The Laser (Light Amplification by Stimulated Emission of Radiation)

Lasers are concentrated _____1 of monochromatic light on the same narrow wavelength. They are one pure _____2, whereas normal light is a _____3 of lightwaves. A laser beam can be concentrated to a _____4 less than one micron, a thousandth of a _____5.

Space _____6 produced a working laser in the 1960s and now they reproduce _____7 from compact discs and are used in supermarket barcode scanners. Excimer lasers used in delicate medical _____8 do not burn surrounding tissues and are used to seal leaking blood _____9—even those in the eyes—or clear clogged arteries. Many _____10 prefer lasers to scalpels as there is less chance of _____11 or bleeding.

In missiles, a laser beam illuminates a _____12 and the missile's detectors home in on the reflected beam of _____13. Such 21st century military developments were even suggested in early _____14, such as when James Bond was threatened with death beams by his _____15 in Goldfinger!

Surveyors can aim lasers at distant buildings with a _____16 calculating the distance from the _____17 taken for the light to return. Scientists are excited about the possible use of lasers to restore the faded _____18 of the 6 000 fragile Chinese terracotta _____19 of Xian without damaging these priceless _____20 from the past.

Use the following adverbs to complete the passage. They are either adverbs of time (e.g. soon, often) or manner (e.g. carefully).

successfully   definitely   passionately   regularly   sometimes   recently
chemically   angrily   expertly   generously   happily   then   wisely
now   carefully   openly   steadily   again   solely   often

Cloning

Dolly the sheep was _____₁ cloned in 1997 and CC (Carbon Copy), the cat, in Texas in 2002. Since then, scientists have _____₂ discussed the possible side-effects of human cloning. Korean researchers _____₃ claimed to have cloned a human embryo but several countries have _____₄ halted such experiments, though a cloned baby was reportedly born in Italy in 2003. US President, George W Bush, once said he was most _____₅ 100% opposed to human cloning. Scientists answer any criticisms _____₆ by claiming they want to use stem cells _____₇ for the problems of disease, injury and old age.

In cloning, the nucleus of a cell from a patient is _____₈ extracted. It is implanted into a donor's denucleated egg cell and _____₉ treated. The embryo soon grows as the cells divide and multiply _____₁₀. The cloned cells can _____₁₁ be implanted into the patient _____₁₂. In experiments so far, the embryos haven't developed far enough for stem cells to be extracted _____₁₃.

Scientists have _____₁₄ obtained stem cells from cloned mouse embryos. However, human experiments are an unpleasant, expensive, and _____₁₅ dangerous procedure for those women who _____₁₆ donate eggs. To obtain eggs _____₁₇, one American cell technology company has _____₁₈ offered donors payments of €3 500 and many have _____₁₉ accepted. Of course, millions of natural clones _____₂₀ roam the Earth—except we call them identical twins!

Use the following words to complete the passage.

dangers   measles   chemicals   died   inserted   bodies   rejected
opposed   deadly   sick   outside   serious   common   groups
available   Africa   centres   drugs   differences   attack

Animal to Human Transplants (Xenotransplantation)

On the _____₁ of human cells are 'marker chemicals' (proteins). If animal cells are put into our _____₂ they are seen as foreign, so our white blood cells _____₃ them. With organ transplants this is called 'rejection' and _____₄ are needed to control it, often with _____₅ side-effects. There are too few human heart donors so genetic engineering scientists have _____₆ human genes into fertilised pig eggs. When each pig matures it has a heart with human marker _____₇. Though patients may die from other causes the scientists believe these hearts would not be _____₈ and could be used until human hearts are _____₉. This could save thousands, perhaps millions, of _____₁₀ patients worldwide.

As diseases like HIV, flu and _____₁₁ appear to have come from animals, there is the risk that a _____₁₂ animal retrovirus could cross to humans, like the dreaded Ebola virus in _____₁₃. Already there are patients who have _____₁₄ shortly after animal organ transplants and critics claim it will be at least a decade before the _____₁₅ are fully realised.

Many church and animal protection _____₁₆ are against further developments, so the location of English research _____₁₇ is secret. There are also cultural _____₁₈ to be faced. Organ transplants between even humans are generally unacceptable in Japan, but _____₁₉ in America and Europe, and some countries are totally _____₂₀ to xenotransplants! Perhaps encouraging more human donors is the answer.

Answers

The Lord of the Rings
Page 1

1. language
2. voted
3. screen
4. Return
5. actors
6. director
7. landscapes
8. found
9. travelling
10. wizard
11. companions
12. destroying
13. journey
14. forces
15. regain
16. creation
17. might
18. again
19. struggle
20. twists

Changing Art
Page 2

1. tombs
2. heroes
3. Romans
4. centuries
5. people
6. museums
7. insurance
8. paintings
9. world
10. film
11. government
12. example
13. paint
14. surface
15. money
16. University
17. lovers
18. complaints
19. room
20. elephants

Child Stars
Page 3

1. famous
2. first
3. successful/popular
4. little
5. humorous
6. youngest
7. British
8. paltry
9. sensible
10. American
11. popular/successful
12. endless
13. annual
14. financial
15. young
16. bitter
17. cheating
18. troubled
19. finest
20. normal

The Family Car
Page 4

1. airbags
2. important
3. experimenting
4. suffers/has
5. safe/specific
6. researched
7. developed
8. message
9. shake/vibrate
10. cost
11. manufactured
12. mixed
13. eventually
14. agreed/begun
15. engines/motors
16. vehicle/car
17. empty
18. view
19. combine
20. companies

Transport in the Future
Page 5

1. differ
2. true
3. moving
4. personal
5. Olympics
6. air
7. private
8. huge
9. called
10. metres
11. down
12. engines
13. weight
14. airports
15. roof
16. litres
17. up
18. deafening
19. cheaper
20. built

Mobile Phones
Page 6

1. palm
2. digital
3. moving
4. using
5. Net/Internet
6. read/interpret
7. pay
8. current
9. form
10. mobile
11. numbers
12. late
13. characters
14. language
15. messages
16. health
17. warned
18. teenagers
19. parents
20. teachers

Bullying
Page 7

1. aware
2. beware
3. names
4. games
5. tall
6. all
7. tease
8. ease
9. choose
10. lose
11. school
12. cruel
13. peers
14. tears
15. TV
16. see
17. rules
18. schools
19. outside
20. denied

Body Image
Page 8

1. indicate/show
2. teachers
3. better
4. apparent/seen
5. ugly
6. beautiful/slim
7. impossible
8. lead
9. dangerous
10. loss
11. two/some
12. school
13. lose
14. said
15. appearance
16. self/body
17. them/children
18. culture
19. around
20. considered

Limited Overs Cricket
Page 9

1. played
2. matches
3. main
4. involved
5. popular
6. part
7. players
8. millions
9. form
10. International
11. colourful
12. critics
13. supporters
14. result
15. different
16. slips
17. third
18. Apart
19. gully
20. three

Extreme Sports
Page 10

1. Extreme
2. physical
3. individual
4. obvious
5. greatest
6. various
7. high-rise
8. dangerous
9. in-line
10. every
11. broken
12. long
13. important
14. firm
15. serious
16. several
17. artificial
18. increasing
19. particular
20. local

Recycling
Page 11

1. paper
2. cartons
3. reduces
4. household
5. required
6. regulations
7. food
8. lifted
9. roads
10. recycled
11. bacteria
12. drunk
13. washes
14. fires
15. supplies
16. technology
17. Europe
18. small
19. find
20. expensive

Robots
Page 12

1. led
2. are
3. produced
4. walked
5. assemble
6. weld
7. programmed
8. approach
9. Equipped
10. searched
11. destroyed
12. driven
13. interacts
14. recognises
15. understand
16. reacts
17. mow
18. find
19. distinguish
20. solve

High-speed Trains
Page 13

1. design
2. steel
3. cables
4. magnetic
5. reached
6. above
7. magnets
8. currents
9. train
10. waves
11. attraction
12. Airport
13. expensive
14. expected
15. England
16. contact
17. silent
18. maintenance
19. power
20. environment

Answers

Exploring the Ocean Depths

Page 14

1. major
2. possible
3. marine
4. useful
5. enormous
6. normal
7. several
8. terrible
9. electric
10. similar
11. American
12. sophisticated
13. amazing
14. popular
15. recent
16. unknown
17. industrial
18. toxic
19. upper
20. lifeless

Protecting Our Borders

Page 15

1. always
2. secretly
3. strictly
4. often
5. cruelly
6. easily
7. recently
8. unsuccessfully
9. obviously
10. adequately
11. heavily
12. possibly
13. badly
14. foolishly
15. horrifyingly
16. gradually
17. specially
18. now
19. Fortunately
20. almost

Global Warming

Page 16

1. emissions
2. temperature
3. support
4. rise
5. populations
6. changes
7. countries
8. India
9. responsible
10. graph
11. thirty-six
12. Japan
13. Canada
14. trees
15. annually
16. earnt
17. paying
18. America
19. country
20. aim

Tectonic Plates – Earthquakes

Page 17

1. millions
2. thick
3. Earth
4. float
5. forced
6. pressures
7. Black
8. north
9. next
10. slowly
11. south
12. illegal
13. buildings
14. damage
15. cartoons
16. safety
17. earthquake
18. Turkey
19. Peru
20. China

Water is Precious

Page 18

1. found
2. lies
3. predicts
4. performed
5. attempted
6. turn
7. provide
8. survive
9. water
10. depend
11. import
12. opened
13. producing
14. possessed
15. put
16. want
17. help
18. soak
19. fix
20. collect

Salinity

Page 19

1. occurs
2. problem
3. years
4. Tigris
5. vegetation
6. available
7. salts
8. Brazil
9. Indonesia
10. areas
11. volunteers
12. remove
13. watertable
14. drainage
15. notice
16. Colorado
17. Egypt/Ethiopia
18. Ethiopia/Egypt
19. China
20. Victoria

Acid Rain

Page 20

1. in England
2. in snow
3. inside homes
4. from volcanoes
5. in the northern hemisphere
6. in fish populations
7. in the water
8. around the world
9. in Europe
10. in many waterways
11. through the air
12. in nearby Germany
13. on monuments
14. from fuels
15. around the local district
16. to affected water
17. in the US Congress
18. in scientific records
19. in Asia
20. in power plants

Genetically Modified (GM) Foods

Page 21

1. dangerous
2. heart
3. concern
4. supermarkets
5. seeds
6. Canada
7. Australia
8. bees
9. grown
10. extra
11. insect
12. tomatoes
13. tastier
14. resistant
15. milk
16. size
17. engineered
18. donated
19. starving
20. protests

Forensic Science

Page 22

1. police
2. successfully
3. programmes
4. clearly
5. types
6. comparison
7. sift
8. analyse
9. stream
10. criminal
11. weapon
12. now
13. phones
14. traced
15. fluids
16. identify
17. cells
18. hair
19. voluntarily
20. others

The Laser

Page 23

1. beams
2. colour
3. mixture
4. point
5. millimetre
6. research
7. music
8. operations
9. vessels
10. surgeons
11. infection
12. target
13. light
14. films
15. enemies
16. computer
17. time
18. colours
19. warriors
20. relics

Cloning

Page 24

1. expertly
2. passionately
3. recently
4. wisely
5. definitely
6. angrily
7. solely
8. carefully
9. chemically
10. steadily
11. then
12. again
13. successfully
14. often
15. sometimes
16. generously
17. regularly
18. openly
19. happily
20. now

Animal to Human Transplants

Page 25

1. outside
2. bodies
3. attack
4. drugs
5. serious
6. inserted
7. chemicals
8. rejected
9. available
10. sick
11. measles
12. deadly
13. Africa
14. died
15. dangers
16. groups
17. centres
18. differences
19. common
20. opposed